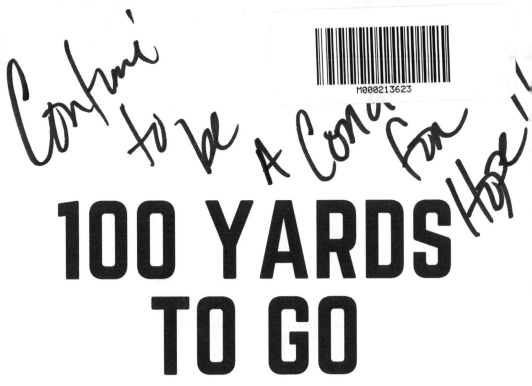

Continue to be A Continue for Hope!

100 YARDS
TO GO

100 Facebook Posts That Will Encourage

Anybody, Especially Former Athletes

By:
Coach DJ Davis

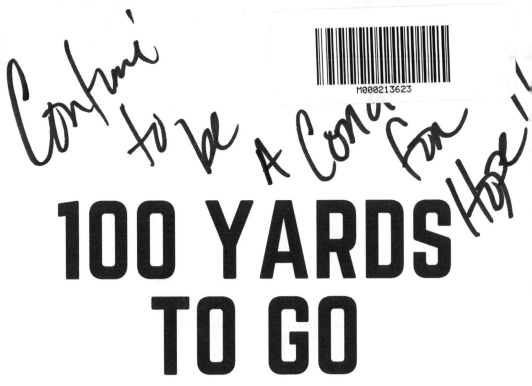

Davis Edupowerment Services, LLC

ISBN: 978-1-7360989-0-5

Editor: Kim Doughty
Book Consultant: Anthony "AJ" Joiner
Cover Design and Typesetting: Katrina Sudario

Davis Edupowerment Services, LLC:
Family-owned and operated business
DeJanai Davis, Chief Executive Officer

Jouhnethan Davis, Vice President
Tosha Davis, Administration
DJ Davis, Community Relations Director

DEDICATED

Larry Jackson 1987

Billy Biggs 1989

Brian Castle 1993

Jim Holland 1996

*"You continue to dream the wild dreams
that you dream when you were young."*

Mike Tomlin,
Head Coach, Pittsburgh Steelers*

What in the Sam Hill would have inspired someone to go through
five year's worth of Facebook posts just to find 100 "good ones"?
Well, I am glad you asked! I want to thank AJ Joiner, The Pub -
lishing King, for sparking this idea. In his Facebook group, Idea
to Book, he asked participants to consider compiling inserts
from journals, blogs, and diaries to create a quick and easy book or
devotional. Well, I figured it only made sense to go back and get
all of my thought-provoking Facebook posts.

I have to be honest and disclaim that the post in this
book are in their original form, and this act was intentional.
Therefore, don't be surprised to see abbreviations, typos, and
slang. I am very confident that this compilation will provide you
with some motivation, some inspiration, and a different perspec -
tive on living. Life can be tough and many of us, including myself
have been beat up by life. It has been a well kept secret that
former athletes, especially males, have a higher degree of difficulty
dealing with life after athletics. Their day-to-day life choices can be interru -
pted by hopelessness, indecisiveness, and worthlessness.

I was that former athlete.

The ex-athlete and former coach in me will always nav
igate toward football's correlation to life. Therefore, the title   -
100 Yards to Go is analogous to the starting and finishing of this
game called life.

We are beginning from the start of one major goal and we will complete a bunch of small goals in progression. We are going from goal to goal and there are 100 goals in between.

We have 100 yards to go, so let us not waste time!

LET'S GO!

Coach DJ Davis

1

Straight from Da Coach's desk: the game clock doesn't start 'til we begin to bless others with what little we have. Until then my friend, we still in the locker room!
#getinthegame

2

Spoke with the director @ DOT and asked why they spent
so much time and energy making sure the roads are lined
with the yellow stripes and reflectors. I noticed how painstakingly
the task was to paint and line the roads. He mentioned
that they wanted to ensure that people stayed in
their lanes and that getting them to their destination was
the most important goal. Think about this next time you
trying to get in someone else's lane and do what they do.
God has spent a lot of time and energy preparing your
road and making sure you get to your destination.
#jrtp #stayinyourlane

3

Don't get it twisted! I am a big supporter of getting that education, whether it's via a degree, a certificate or some form of licensing—go get it!? But realize that those are just enhancements to the true gift! The gift is what will make room for you so don't get tied up with the paperwork Just do the work! #thenewjrtp

4

I'm thankful for the good and not so good things going on in my life right now. They both allow me to realize how small I am in relationship to His mercy and grace.

5

"You will never know what's on the other side of a single sheet of paper until you flip it over. Stop living a one dimensional, one-sided, flat-life. Flip yourself! You may be surprised what you'll find on the other side."

6

When you get the confirmation, confirmation is confirmation. There is now way around it, can't avoid it!

7

A light doesn't shine until a switch has been turned on so don't assume just because you are a light people are going to automatically see your shine. Turn yourself on.

#jrtp

8

A lot of emphasis and concern about the confederate flag and the LGBT flag. Some of ya'll need to focus on buying some Black Flag. #willgooversomeofyallhead #jokes #debugyourminds #pestcontrol #SPRAYAROUNDYOUROWNSTEPSANDCABINET SANDBEDROOM

9

Everybody needs that opportunity to regroup.
#checkcheck #omaha!

10

Shoulda made a left at Albuquerque!!

1st Down!

Shoulda Made A Left At Albuquerque!

—— The Motivation ——

We have all been there! We have made a decision and then midway following the decision, we realize we have made the wrong one! We have done it once and I do be lieve we will do it again! Do not fret! Even our old friend Bugs Bunny was famous for-realizing he had made a det rimental mistake in trying to escape from Elmer Fudd. He would confirm his mistake by saying he, "shoulda made a left at Albuquerque." In the end, Bugs would find a way to overcome his "wrong turn" and so shall we!

11

Due to generational curses, (read Genesis and about Abraham) most—not all of us, are behind a lap or two in the areas of finances, marital and spiritual relationships, family bonding, being real fathers, and other vices. First we have to recognize it's a curse and then use Galatians 3:13 to allow us to catch up and overcome those curses and don't allow it to be an excuse.

12

Before we began to judge people who are less fortunate
than we are, or not as "christian" as us, remember we are all one
bad decision from being homeless, broke, on
drugs, in an affair etc. Humble thyselves and make
somebody's day this Easter weekend.

13

It aint over 'til He say it is. So imma keep pulling my jumper from the arc.

14

"Trying to keep up will get you caught up"—the things that pop up in my head..

#leavethejonesesalone #doyou

15

If you have never done it, quit trying to tell people how to do it. Give them the name and number of someone you know who has done it.

16

Is there such a thing as being at the right place at the wrong time or wrong place at the right time? If so, explain your answer.

17

Remember, there are usually 4 sides to every story.

18

Shadows only exist because the Light wants them to.

19

Sometimes it's just best to grab ya kahunas with both hands, close your eyes, jump, and yell Geronimo!
#whatsworsecanhappen

20

Hard as it is for me to do cuz its not in my makeup. When no other options are available, the best thing I can do is just sit and be patient. #allotheroptionsarefutile #stillintraining #thatleoinme

1st Down!

Hard as it is for me to do cuz it's not in my makeup. When no other options are available, the best thing I can do is just sit and be patient.

—— The Motivation ——

They tell us that patience is virtue? I have an "A" personal - ity type and I tend to focus more on the results than I do the steps that get me to the results. This action oriented style can sometimes lead to making decisions based on impulse. Patience has the ability to allow us to see exactly what we need to see to make right decisions. It is a virtue.

21

PSA: we all deserve to be here, planet earth that is, but what we do with the time here is what separates us.

#purposedfilledlives #stopwastingtime

22

One thing I learned as a Coach is if you give a man a play you expect him to run the play you gave him. As a veteran I can see what he can't see. I have earned the right to call the play. The problem in our community is we got too many rookies trying to tell veterans how to play the game. #jrtp

23

In these times of Google, Snapchat, and Bing, society has been tricked to believe you can get from point A to C without having to go thru point B. Unfortunately it has caused our young people to feel a sense of entitlement and they don't understand how to respond to the slightest est adversity. As a Coach, I have learned that we can't win game 6 if we haven't played game 3. Let's begin to teach our young people about adversity and that taking short cuts only creates bigger, deeper cuts. #jrtp #play9

24

Even in tennis, an individual sport, superb players such as Serena William still have a team of people who work together to get her to her best peak performances.

25

I've heard the saying
"It's lonely at the top".

26

So hot outside I got my sunscreen
on inside the house.

27

Can you be awesome and average at the same time?

28

I think too many options can be detrimental to the decision making process. We think we want options but sometimes our wants and needs become convoluted in a cloud of indecisiveness. I looked at all this cold and cough medicine and almost forgot what symptoms I had. Life: know what you want. Pick a play. Run it! #jrtp #mtc #keepmyoptionstoaminimum

29

If you spend more than 30 minutes in a conversation with a person and at the least one of you didn't get any thing from the convo that will help you/them (job info, life skills, spiritual, networking info, recipe, something!) then y'all would have done better not talking at all.

30

There are two types of motivation: intrinsic and extrinsic. Our society has us more focused on one than the other. With big contracts like the one Dez Bryant just signed, it's easy for our young athletes to get caught up in the idea that if "I can't get a big reward then it must not be worth it." One of the motivations says that I am willing to do the work regardless of what I get. Which one do you focus on? #jrtp

1st Down!

There are two types of motivation:
intrinsic and extrinsic

The Motivation

By the time I became a senior in high school there were
not too many people in the town that did not know who
I was. We were not only the first team to set many goals,
we also won the 1st state championship! I had all the out -
side motivation I needed to be successful. Fast-forward to
college and those same outside motivators were not as
frequent as they were in the past. I was a walk-on. I did not
have colleges knocking down my door to recruit me. I be   -
came a walk-on who turned starter and had to pull from
every ounce of intrinsic motivation I had! Remember in life
there will be times that you will be your only fan, but that
one fan will be enough to see you through!

31

Descriptive acts do not have the same effect as active acts.
Do sometime active today and not just talk about it. #mtc #jrtp

32

We bite off more than we can chew
and then mad when we get choked.

33

Waiting on God to open some doors, huh? Well, He waiting on you to kick some down. #jrtp

34

Count all of it joy.
All of it.

35

Sometimes to make good decisions you have to be around people who make good decisions. #jrtp

36

"Sometimes the right hand don't need to know what the left hand doing."—Mrs. Eura Dell Davis

37

Don't let anybody be better than you today!
#jrtp

38

We conscientiously deal with Chevy Impala-type people
but get pissed off when they can't do Bugatti-type performances

#jrtp #chevyvsbugatti #mtc #choosewisely
#atoasterwillneverbeamicrowave
#amicrowavewillneverbeatelevision

39

Somebody needs to really take time to say, "God, my Cre
ator, and Master Manufacturer, this is   .
I am ready to be what you made me to be. I am willing to
take whatever steps necessary to be the best me I can be.
Yes, just like many machines or products manufactured by
man, I have been dropped, misused, under-appreciated,
and mishandled. But as of today, I am still capable of being
the exact thing I was made for. Give me my instruction
manual now so I can be good at being great. Thank you
for the tools and parts you gave me to shine and be suc
cessful in the purpose you have made me for. Amen." Say
that everyday at least 1x for 28 days and see what happens.
Come back to this post and comment your results below.

#jrtp

40

Water is considered the universal solvent. It has the ability to change properties depending on its temperature and environment. It can go from a solid, liquid, or gas. Water, from a molecular standpoint has the ability to do whatever it needs to do to be whatever it needs to be. We are made of about 70% of this same water but allow 30% of the other stuff to keep us from doing what we need to do to be what we need to be. #jrtp

1st Down!

Water is considered the universal solvent.

The Motivation

We have everything we need already in us to be what we were designed to be. This post was motivated by a con - versation I had with a coworker who was allowing outside influences to impact their abilities to be successful. The amount of outside influences regardless of how big they may seem will never be high enough to overcome the internal mechanisms that are already interlaced within.

41

I have no problem being the saucer under the cup.

42

Some of y'all allowing your Day 1s
to waste your whole day.

43

Pray for those who have to carry
anchors they didn't purchase.

44

Sometimes being productive isn't about what you can create but what you say to others that inspire them to create.

#jrtp

45

It's me versus me. Everything and everybody else is just practice.

46

Your next breakthrough is buried deep
in the soil of consistency.

47

I don't have a problem proving myself. Been doing it since about 1976.

48

Not asking for what you need: 100% No.
Asking for what you need: +50% Yes.
Shoot your shot!

49

We all have a little bit of, "I can't wait to prove these bastards wrong" in us! Some of us just decide to act on it, some of us don't!

50

Some of y'all can be watching Get Smart on a smartphone eating Smarties and drinking Smart water and still do dumb sutff.

1st Down!

Some of y'all can be watching Get Smart on a smart phone
eating Smarties and drinking Smart water
and still do dumb stuff.

The Motivation

This post can be in correlation with the Yard 40 post. We
cannot allow all the tools we have been equipped with, the
tools we have picked up along this journey called life, and
the useful people in our lives, to go to waste or be in vain
because we are not focused. We have everything we need.

51

You are waaaaay better than you think you are. Try your self out and see what happens. #jrtp

52

Just because you and your crew on the dance floor together doesn't mean y'all dancing to the same beat. #jrtp

53

We all need subtle reminders (people and events) to remind us never to settle for mediocrity.

54

Don't wake up one day and regret you didn't risk it all.
That you didn't even take a chance.

55

Mrs. Eura Dell always told me that if at all possible, leave stuff better than you found it.

56

Don't assume a mentor has to be older than you. There are a lot of younger people out here we can learn from.

57

Be open minded to what Destiny has to say.
She knows what she is talking about.

58

Just because a toaster is scratched up and has a dent in it doesn't mean it can't still be a great toaster.

59

The journey to greatness shouldn't be traveled alone.
Let's do it together. Don't follow me—join me.

60

You got the revelation but you still sitting at the station.

1st Down!

You got the revelation but you still sitting at the station.

—— The Motivation ——

You can have all the potential in the world and no action behind it makes it just that...potential. You have been told many times that you are ready. God has done everything but come back down in the flesh to remind you that you are ready. Ready for what? Ready to live the life you are supposed to. How many times does the rescue boat have to pass by you before you drown?

61

Everybody want Cadillac but don't want to pay the note!

62

When you were made the batteries were included.
When will you start acting like it?!!

63

Is not making a decision just as bad as making a bad one?

64

Even the largest seed is small compared to the tree it pro
duces. Keep digging. Keep planting. Your small is big.

65

Insecurity is the key ingredient in Doubt cake—will have you doubting everything and everybody. Mainly yourself. #donteatthecakeanniemae #justruntheplay

66

A shepherd with no vision
will soon be sheepless. #jrtp

67

You've been scooting to the edge
of your purpose too long.

68

It is OK to be ordinary when God
has given you an extraordinary.

69

You are one "believe" away from your breakthrough. Who you believing in?? Don't allow you to be your only opposition—get out of your own way! #jrtp

70

Regardless of how big or small the load, I will not drop any clothes when getting them out the dryer in 2020!

1st Down!

Regardless of how big or small the load, I will not drop any clothes when getting them out the dryer in 2020!

—— **The Motivation** ——

As funny as this post may be it does have a life learning lesson associated with it. We have to establish some non-negotiables in life if we expect to see any success. What worked for you last year may not work for you this year. Make a decision to refuse to lose. Do not drop the socks!

71

Build your own yellow brick road.

72

I have not put on any cologne or body spray since March 13th. Bruh man, just wiping down in hand sanitizer and backarub.

73

Stop being bitter, just get better.

74

Would you rather live your life in a straight line? Or with crescendos and decrescendos?

75

It is a proven principle: you speak into the atmosphere... it's going to happen! This God guy is fashionably on time!

76

I just heard my grandma voice, "I don't care what virus out there, you ain't going to be in and out that kitchen doing all that progin'!"

77

Stop looking crazy at people who have big ideas in a small world! You may have to apply to work for them one day!

78

The mind is a terrible thing to waste epecially
when you are spending too much time thinking
about how to be a good toaster, when it is obvious
God made you to be the greatest microwave!

79

If your mind is not right,
nothing else will be.

80

Stay hungry! So when they try to feed
you the crumbs, you still make a meal out of it!!!

1st Down!

Stay hungry! So when they try to feed you the crumbs you still make a meal out of it!

The Motivation

Complacency is a purpose killer! Just because you arrived does not mean you will survive. You have to treat each opportunity as if it was your last. Always be ready, stay ready. Be ready to make the most of any situation. There will be times when you will be given the short hand of the stick. Play that hand!

81

Sometimes you have to digress in order to invest, so progress is neccessary.

82

You're praying. They are working.
There is a difference.

83

There is a difference between your job and your work.
Which one do you focus more on?

84

Some of ya'll seek success but have not considered or thought about a successor.

85

For those of you who don't think being around the right person/people is important, ask them dudes who were in that boat with Paul.

86

Any of you plan on becoming
great you best be ready to serve.

87

Want power? Get purpose!

88

Stop looking and begin to seek.

89

You have all day today.
Do something that rises you above the norm.

90

I don't know who needs to hear this, but stop working harder on a job than you are on yourself.

1st Down!

—— Yard 90 ——

I don't know who needs to hear this, but stop working harder on a job than you are on yourself.

The Motivation

I was talking with a friend about one of his coworkers. His coworker had recently passed away and his position was filled within two weeks after his funeral. It did not surprise me to hear this because that is how the Just Over Broke has treated people for years. To loosely paraphrase a verse in the Bible, "What does it profit a man to gain a good job, but lose a greater sense of self?"

91

Progress is painful. Ask ya momma!
#ninemonths

92

Before you can say it, you have to have seen or had a vision. It's hard to say what you hadn't seen and it's hard to seal what you can't say.

Write the vision
There is power in the tongue
Seal it and make it official (Daniel 6)

93

Purpose will always lead to productivity
which will lead to profit.

94

Momma would say, "Be industrious, not ignant. Anybody can be ignant."

95

The pessimists complain; the optimists expect change; the real ones just make adjustments.

96

I have accomplished a lot on this journey my past two years, but there is so much more that needs to be done. All distractions are temporary and so is pain. Pride is forever.

97

Blessings are like flowers and plants. Some come like roses real quick and make an immediate impact but are short lived. Others come like oak trees.. Take forever to get here but once they take root they last forever.

98

Momma would say, "Son ya gotta look out for #1." Why? You are your only guarantee; nothing or no one else is.

99

She would also say, "Use ya head for more than just a hatrack."

100

Don't stop until you are under 99 rocks.

1st Down!

Don't stop until you are under 99 rocks.

The Motivation

The only thing that can stop you from succeeding
here on Earth is you and death. "99 rocks" represent the
layers of soil that is placed over a casket during burial.
Set a goal, plan, plot, strategize, and then execute.
You have no excuse to not make it to the top.
Death will come to visit us all, but until he does...LIVE!

Thank you. You did not have to spend money or time on this project, but you did. I pray that the money, time, and energy spent finds its way back to you in a multiplying manner.

Davis Edupowerment Services, LLC takes forward progress personally. That is why we decided to invite you to experience some of Coach DJ's most personal thoughts and feelings. I pray that you found at least one post that positively changed the way you see yourself and your world.

We are forever grateful to those who have been supportive since day one. My heart is big enough for all of you!

—DeJanai Davis, President, DES

TABLE OF POSTS AND THEIR THEMES

Post	First Words	Theme
1	Straight from the	Supporting others
2	Spoke with the	Mind yourself
3	Don't get it twisted!	Dedications
4	I'm thankful for the	Humble yourself, relationship with God
5	"You will never know	"One dimensional life"
6	When you get the	Confirmation
7	A light doesn't shine	Supporting self
8	A lot of emphasis	Conflict
9	Everybody needs that	Regroup
10	Shoulda made a left	Decisions

47	I don't have a problem	Proving self
48	NOT asking for	Taking care of self, Ask for what is needed
49	We all have a little bit	Proving others wrong, Differences among people
50	Some of y'all can be watching	Illusion of intelligence, "Dumb" decisions
51	You are waaaaaay better	Trust yourself
52	Just because you and your crew	Motivations, Differences amongst people,
53	We all need subtle reminders	Don't settle for mediocrity, outside support
54	Don't wake up one day	Regret, taking chances
55	Mrs. Eura Dell	Improvement, Mrs. Eura Dell
56	Don't assume a mentor	Assumptions, Mentoring
57	Be open minded to what	Destiny, Open-Mindedness
58	Just because a toaster	Imperfections, Functionality

71	Build ya own yellow	Supporting self
72	I have not put on any	COVID-19, "Essentials"
73	Stop being bitter,	Get over defeat, dedications
74	Would u rather live	Life's path
75	It is a proven principle	Trust God's plan
76	I just heard my grandma	Mrs. Eura Dell
77	Stop looking crazy at people who	Support "idea" people
78	The mind is a terrible thing to waste	Trusting God's plan/purpose
79	If your mind if not right	Keep your mind right; taking care of self
80	Stay hungry!	Making the most out of little
81	Sometimes you have to digress	Progress
82	You're praying....	Putting in work, Dedication

References

*"Mike Tomlin 2008 commencement speech at St. Vincent College one of NPR's 300 best of all time" by Bryan DeArdo,

www.behindthesteelcurtain.com
June 1, 2014.